THE ALMERÍA COAST

THE
ALMERÍA
COAST

Essay and photographs
LUCAS VALLECILLOS

TRIANGLE ▼ POSTALS

THE ALMERÍA COAST

The coast of Almería stretches between the provinces of Murcia and Granada in eastern Andalusia, just at the point where the Mediterranean fuses the south and El Levante together. The climate here is warm and dry as a result of the limited rainfall but high level of sunshine throughout the year. The average temperatures are around 13°C in winter and 25°C in summer, making it possible to enjoy the beaches virtually all year round. This long coastline, full of remarkable landscapes, white villages, watchtowers and fortresses built in the past to provide a defence against pirate raids, is structured around the city of Almería, the chief city and the political, financial and cultural capital of the province.

To the east of this city, if we ignore the developed area of Vera and Garrucha, is the El Levante coast, which has the most spectacular beaches of the entire Almería shoreline, with the best kept secrets to be found in the Cabo de Gata-Níjar Natural Park. In the park, there are wide-open spaces to be enjoyed, with numerous hidden beaches and coves where you can savour a sense of solitude. Many places can only be reached on foot, making it a paradise for nature lovers and keen walkers.

Even though they have no coastline, there are three spots that we have decided to include in this book because of their outstanding beauty and their proximity to the sea. So exceptional are these places that they cannot go unnoticed by the traveller visiting the Almería coast. One of these is the municipality of Sorbas, which has a wealth of history and a remarkable natural setting that includes one of the most important gypsum karst formations in the world, offering countless potholing possibilities. Another is the Tabernas Desert, the only area that meets all the

◄ San José

scientific conditions of a desert in Europe. The wanderer will feel like a veritable cowboy in the loneliness of this enigmatic, almost magical landscape that resembles those found in the US states of Nevada and Arizona. And the third of these remarkable spots is the Almerian Alpujarra, consisting of a group of villages on the southern side of the Sierra Nevada. Of all the surprises that a trip along the coast of Almería and its neighbouring lands holds in store for the traveller, this is the least expected of all: the subdesert plantlife and climate along the coast become high mountain vegetation and weather in barely a few kilometres.

To the west of Almería is the El Poniente coast, with the most developed tourist resorts in the province, including Roquetas de Mar, Aguadulce and Almerimar. These towns have everything that a tourist on a classic beach holiday could require.

One highly characteristic feature along the entire coast that will draw the outsider's eye, though not because of their beauty, are the huge swathes of land given over to greenhouses: vast seas of plastic responsible for turning the province of Almería into the largest vegetable producing area in the world. This, together with tourism, is the miracle that has turned an extremely poor area —a region so impoverished that its population was forced to leave in search of a better life— into a prosperous land that provides employment for a considerable number of immigrants. The European Union's experts in agriculture regard Almería as the vegetable garden of Europe.

Roquetas ▸

Almería may not number among the cities in Andalusia with the most monuments and sites, but it would be a mistake to underestimate its worth. It has more than enough charms to capture the heart of the discriminating traveller. To wend your way around Almería is to penetrate the passing of time, it is to experience the peace and tranquillity of a small provincial city, it is to enjoy the traditional ritual of sampling tapas, to feel the warmth of the people of Almería, but above all, it is to delight in a Mediterranean city that enjoys its relationship with the sea to the full.

THE CITY

The origins of Almería are to be found in al-Andalus, in the 10th century, to be precise, when Abd al-Rahman III, having annexed the wealthy Republic of Pechina to the Caliphate of Cordoba, decided to fortify the maritime quarter of Pechina in order to defend against Fatimid invasions. There he had built the impressive Alcazaba that stands in its commanding position, looking out over the city. And so it was that al-Mariya Bayyana was born and came to acquire great splendour during the period of Muslim rule. Its port became the most important in the caliphate. It was the main harbour for the fleet of the Cordovan army and a busy commercial hub. Through its docks vast quantities of goods were moved, among them fabrics and marble from Macael on their way to other continents. The port area was transformed into what was effectively a large city with walls that extended to encompass almost a million square metres and which had more than 15 gates. The medina spread alongside the Alcazaba and in the Church of Sant Juan it is still possible to see the mihrab of the great mosque. The wealth that flooded into the city was such that two important suburbs grew up around it: El Aljibe, where the popular neighbourhood of La Chanca is to be found today; and La Musalla, formerly home to the souk, which stretched from Calle Reina to Plaza Vieja. Apart from a ten year period in the mid-12th century (1147-1157) due to a Christian incursion ordered by Alfonso VII of Castile and supported by Pope Eugene III, this golden age lasted until 1489, when the city finally fell to the Catholic Monarchs.

Under the Christians, Almería not only underwent a dramatic change in its urban landscape due to the construction of many new churches and the transformation of all the existing mosques into churches and their minarets into bell towers, but also entered a mediocre period in its history,

*« View of the city from
Cerro de San Cristóbal
‹ The La Chanca
neighbourhood*

its worst moments being a series of devastating earthquakes such as those of 1518 and 1522. This last earthquake practically destroyed the city and is responsible for the fact that no other monuments from al-Mariya Bayyana's rich past have survived. In contrast, the new Christian constructions were repaired and even improved. A good example of this is the cathedral, which originally occupied the Church of San Juan, since it was rebuilt on its original site and made considerably grander than the original. It was not until the 19th century that Almería emerged from the its economic and cultural decline into the beginnings of a new era of splendour. The growth in mining and the trade in grapes from Berja and Ohanes had an impact on the entire province and filled the port once again with a continuous flow of goods that in turn created a rising bourgeoisie that then made sweeping changes to the architectural shape of the city and to its social life. Impressive constructions were erected as a result of this boom in the late 19th and early 20th centuries, consisting of the infrastructure needed for the economy to grow, and civil buildings to meet the needs of an increasingly wealthy elite, including the Casino Cultural, the Teatro Cervantes, the Archbishop's Palace, the ore loading track and jetty known as the Cable Inglés, the Central Market and the railway station. Almería continued to expand eastwards until it came to form the city we see today, a city that hosted the Mediterranean Olympics in 2005 and which, in its Rambla de Belén, Paseo Marítimo, Mediterranean Stadium, Maestro Padilla Auditorium, Intermodal Station, Art Centre and Archaeological Museum, has all the modern facilities required to successfully meet the challenges of the future.

View of the port ›
from La Alcazaba

The Jayrán Walls ‣

▲ *La Alcazaba, the Torre del Homenaje keep*

La Alcazaba,
Torre de los Espejos

The La Chanca ›
neighbourhood and
La Alcazaba

The cathedral
‹ *The high altar*
The Door of Forgiveness ›

▴ *The town hall*

Bodega Las Botas ▸
Local cuisine ▸

‣ *Monument to the 142 Almerians who died in the Mauthausen concentration camp*

Railway station ‣
Rambla de Belén ‣

The Cable Inglés jetty ▸

▴ *Fishing port*

Muelle de Levante jetty ▸
Playa del Zampillo ▸

TABERNAS DESERT AND THE SIERRA ALHAMILLA

These two spaces make up a mysterious landscape that has illuminated dreams and unleashed the imagination of numerous filmmakers who have used it as a location for their productions. In its heyday, above all during the 1960s, film had a golden epoch here that has never been repeated with quite the same splendour. Not only is the Tabernas Desert remarkable in its appearance, but its environmental conditions are unique in Europe.

TABERNAS DESERT

Between the impressive mountainous masses of the Sierra Alhamilla to the south, the Sierra Nevada to the west and the Sierra de los Filabres to the north lies the Tabernas Desert in an area isolated from the wet currents of the Mediterranean and lashed by the constant scourge of extremely dry air, creating the very harsh atmospheric conditions typical of a desert climate. The average temperature all year is around 17ºC, rainfall barely reaches 300 litres per square metre and sunshine amounts to 3,000 hours. This combination of meteorological conditions is unique in Europe and is being exploited by the innovative Almería Solar Platform run by CIEMAT, the largest centre in the world researching and developing concentrated solar radiation technologies.

The Tabernas Desert is a depression with soil consisting of saline clays and marl. Annual rainfall here is extremely low, though torrential downpours may occur in spring and autumn. Given the scant plantlife, rain runoffs can cause considerable erosion damage and the main gullies fill with fast-flowing water that drag matter down towards the sea. Paradoxically, water is the principal agent that shapes this desert, giving rise to an extraordinary landscape, known scientifically as 'badlands', made up of gullies, ditches, ravines, torrent courses and extremely arid plateaus. The limited flora and fauna are concentrated in the gullies and ravines, where there is a certain dampness in the ground due to springs produced by a very high water table. This territory became a vast film set in the 1960s to 80s due to its close resemblance to the deserts of north America. It all began when the Italian film director Sergio Leone set foot in the Almerian desert to make his first film, his intention being to cut down on the costs that filming on the other side of the big pond would have entailed.

« Rambla de Tabernas and the spot known as La Tortuga
‹ Tabernas

And so emerged the sub-genre known as 'spaghetti westerns', Spanish and Italian co-productions that include classics such as *A Fistful of Dollars* and *For a Few Dollars More*. In recent times, the area has been used in the main for shooting adverts, though some films have been made on location here, among them *800 Bullets* by Alex de la Iglesia.

The town that the desert is named after is also worth visiting, above all for the Church of Nuestra Señora de la Encarnación and the remains of a Nasrid castle. From its battlements 80 metres up, you can admire the entire town of Tabernas and make out the Sierra Alhamilla in the distance.

▾ Rambla de Tabernas　　　　　　　　　　　　　　　　　　　　　*Tabernas Castle ▸*

‹ *Rambla de Tabernas*

39

‹ Salts deposited on Rambla de Tabernas
by mineral-rich waters

▲ The Tabernas Desert

‹ *Rambla de Tabernas*

▴ *Almería Solar Platform,*
managed by CIEMAT

43

Oasys, Park of the Desert of Taverns. Spaghetti western sets ▴ ▸

SIERRA ALHAMILLA

There is no better way to complete an excursion through the desert than climbing the Sierra Alhamilla. This splendid natural area has indigenous woodland and forests with stunted holm oaks and very mature pines, and offers spectacular views out over the Tabernas badlands on the north face and the Cabo de Gata to the south. The foothills at the very bottom of the sierra are scattered with extremely interesting villages, such as Lucainena de las Torres and Turrillas, and a welcoming spa known as the Baños de Sierra Alhamilla. The spring that feeds the spa was enjoyed by the Phoenicians, Romans and above all the Arabs. The water issues from the ground at 58ºC and is rich in sodium carbonate and calcium chloride and is good for treating digestive, bone and respiratory disorders.

▼ *Holm oak*   *Turrillas* ▸

▲ *Turrillas, the Shrine of St. Anthony of Padua*

▲ *Cortijo del Saltador*

▴ *House on Rambla Honda*

Baños de Sierra Alhamilla spa ▸

ALMERIAN ALPUJARRA

This is the least known side of Almería and perhaps by virtue of being so unexpected, it tends to impress the most. The towns and villages here have managed to develop extremely tastefully and have never forgotten their roots, which has kept them untainted by the property speculation suffered along the coast. After the Arabs were expelled from Granada, they came and lived here for a hundred years, stamping their mark on every corner of the territory.

The vast region of La Alpujarra is usually associated in people's minds with the province of Granada. Yet this legendary district respects no political boundaries and its towns extend into the land of Almería as well. Much smaller than the area of La Alpujarra that lies in the province of Granada, the Almerian Alpujarra has almost all of its municipalities scattered along the fertile valley of the Andarax River, between the Sierra Nevada and the Sierra de Gádor. Calm reigns supreme here, as does a lifestyle that refuses to turn its back on the past, it still being possible to see men working with a plough drawn by an animal, the only way to gain access to the terraced farmland and to move heavy loads around here. The towns and villages in this area have a rich historical heritage, with grand houses that were built by the Christians following the Reconquest, remains of Arab edifices, magnificent Baroque fountains and a number of highly interesting parish churches. These and the outstanding natural surroundings are well worth an unhurried visit to enjoy their charms to the full.

One of the most surprising things to the eyes of a visitor from the coast, apart from the sudden change in landscape and climate, is the marvellous architecture of La Alpujarra. Towns and villages follow a tortuous line, with their narrow streets of a markedly North African character, hugging the hillsides on which they stand and giving rise to places of extreme beauty. Houses in La Alpujarra are externally unlike those elsewhere in Almería because of their roofs, which are grey in colour and made of *launa* (mica schist), an impermeable material that copes well with the harsh winters in the area, and which are topped by an unusual chimney with a slab of slate set horizontally across the top in the manner of a hat. The finest example of this local architecture is to be found in Ohanes, whose delicious grapes were exported around the entire world via the port in Almería.

« *Ohanes*
‹ *Ohanes*

▴ *The environs of Ohanes*

▲ Grape-picking in Ohanes

Terraced land near Canjáyar ➤
Fruit of the land ➤

▴ *Ohanes. Leading goats towards pastureland*

▲ *Ohanes. Saddling up a donkey*

‹ *Bayárca*   ‹ *Shepherd near Fondón*

▴ *Pilar Seco in Laujar de Andarax*

▲ *Women gathering almonds near Ohanes*

Ohanes

Ohanes

THE PONIENTE COAST

Adra, Almerimar, Roquetas de Mar, Aguadulce and the Punta Entinas-Sabinar Nature Reserve are the main attractions on this stretch of shoreline, which extends to the west of the capital. Even though the entire Almerian coast has turned over to tourism, El Poniente is the area that has most enthusiastically embraced this economic sector. It has excellent facilities and can provide all the services required to ensure visitors can enjoy a fantastic holiday by the sea.

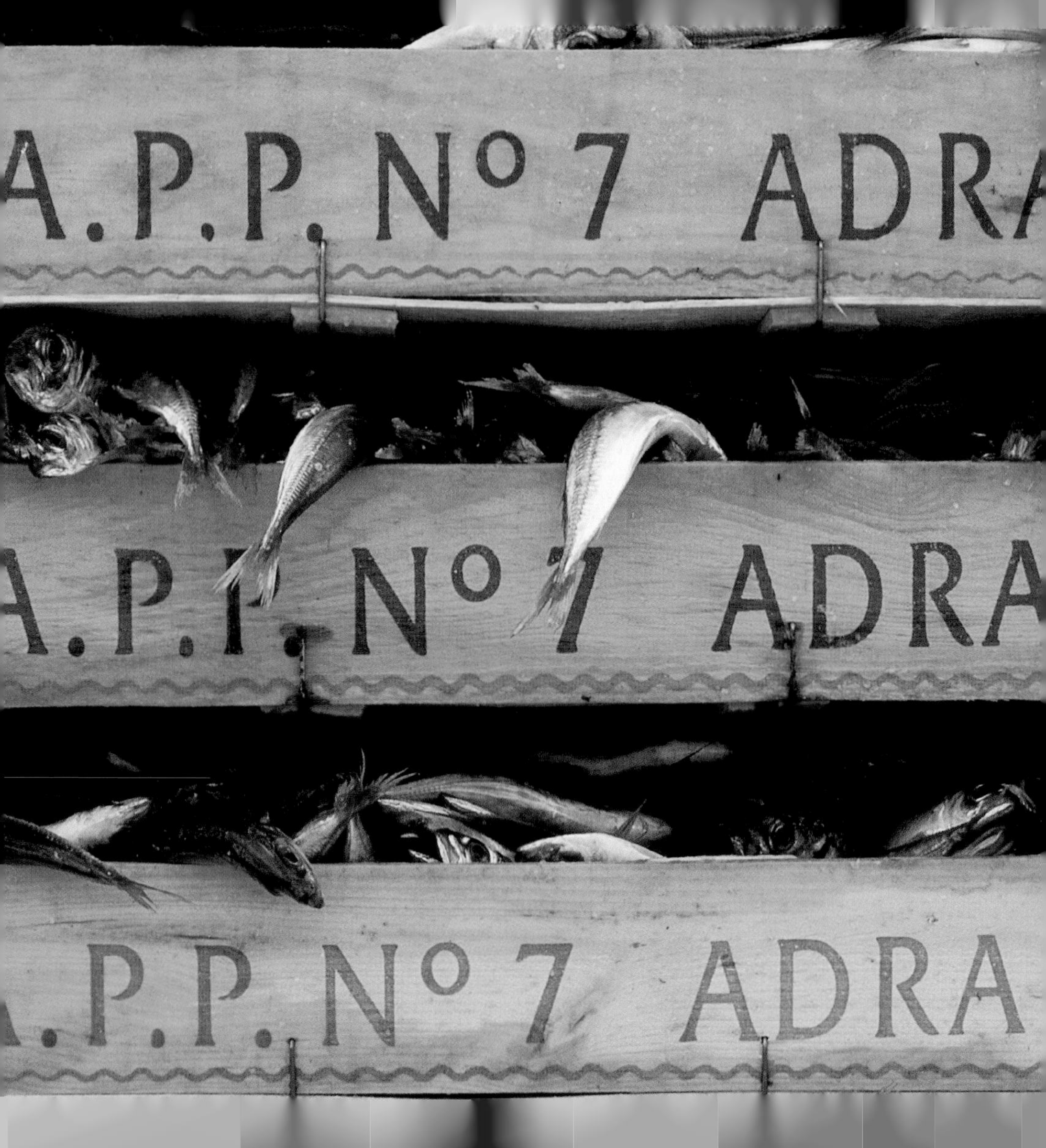
A.P.P. Nº 7 ADRA
A.P.P. Nº 7 ADRA
A.P.P. Nº 7 ADRA

ADRA

The history of this locality dates back to the time of the Phoenicians, its founders. It later passed into the hands of the Romans, Visigoths and Muslims. During the Middle Ages, continuous pirate raids on the towns and villages along the coast resulted in most of the inhabitants deciding to move inland, where they built what is now the quarter of La Alquería. Adra was thus divided into two population centres until 1505, when Queen Juana I ordered that a fortress be built in the original village, prompting much of the population to move back to the coast. The town's most recent past has been prosperous thanks to the wealth generated by the Fundición de Plomo San Andrés, a lead foundry, and by sugar cane production. Adra's economy today is based on greenhouse agriculture, tourism and fishing.

‹ ▾ *Unloading the catch*

« *Adra. Playa de Poniente*

‹ Fishing port
Torre de los Perdigones ›

‣ *Port*

▴ *Entrance to the port*

‹ ▴ *Albuferas de Adra*

ALMERIMAR

This vast development, created exclusively for holiday leisure activities, lies in a truly outstanding natural setting in a cove between Punta de los Baños and Punta de las Entinas. Everything here revolves around golf and a large marina with a capacity of a thousand berths. This is nirvana for modern sea dogs looking for adventure while keeping their backs well covered, and for lovers of the sport that made Severiano Ballesteros famous.

In addition, visitors to Almerimar can enjoy a wide range of hotels, apartments, restaurants, cocktail bars, discotheques and other activities such as diving, fishing, sailing and tennis.

‹ *View*

‹ *Fisherman*

Playing golf ›

THE NATURAL BEAUTY SPOT OF PUNTA ENTINAS-SABINAR

This natural beauty spot covers 1,960 hectares, 785 of which have been declared a nature reserve, along a coastal strip that is 1 kilometre wide and 14 long. The lie of the land is marked by a succession of almost virgin beaches with a long strip of dunes anchored by very dense savin juniper and lentiscus scrub, dotted with wetlands and the large pool formed by the Viejas and Cerrillos saltworks. This landscape provides the perfect environmental conditions for water fowl that come here to rest during their migrations.

‹ *Cerrillos saltworks*

▾ *Large house near the Cerrillos saltworks*

▴ *Torre de Cerrillos*

Punta Sabinar lighthouse ›
Old water lift at the Cerrillos ›
saltworks

ROQUETAS DE MAR AND AGUADULCE

A number of different peoples passed through these lands in ancient times, but it was during the al-Andalus period that Roquetas de Mar acquired a status of its own in history due to the construction of a fortress on the site where the Santa Ana Castle today stands. A permanent village grew up around this fortress and eventually developed into the most important town in the province after the chief city itself. Roquetas has one of the most modern bullrings in Andalusia and an auditorium with a futurist design that hosts major artistic productions.

The city's economy is based on agriculture—the people here were the first in Almería to erect a greenhouse—and tourism, which is concentrated around the Aguadulce marina and the leisure services and activities in the immediate surroundings.

▾ The port lighthouse

The auditorium ▸

Playa de Aguadulce

‹ *Playa del Rompillo*

▲ *Playa la Ventilla*

‹ *Castle of Santa Ana*   ‚ *Playa de la Bajadilla*

Bullring ◂ ▸

THE LEVANTE COAST

This stretch of shoreline extends to the east of the chief city from Punta del Santo to San Juan de los Terreros, the gates of the province of Murcia. Even though this area has not escaped the fierce property speculation that has ravaged the coast, it is, after Cabo de Gata, the place with the most unspoiled and attractive beaches in the whole of Almería. In addition, it has Mojácar, regarded as the paradigm of the Andalusian village.

MOJÁCAR

Until the 1960s, the people of Mojácar had very little to do with the sea and virtually ignored its presence. The arrival of tourism, however, entailed a huge transformation of the town's seafront that is still continuing to this day and which means that the populace now has a close relationship with the Mediterranean. As a result of this change, Mojácar is divided into two very distinctive parts: the old part of the town, which is approximately 1 kilometre from the coast, and the area that developed around the beaches.

The town of Mojácar, like every other true Andalusian town, wends its way up a hillside, in this case at the northern end of the Sierra Cabrera, and experienced a highpoint in its history under Arab rule. The spring, now a fountain known as Fuente de los Doce Caños or Fuente Mora that has twelve spouts, was undoubtedly what drew the first human settlers here to build a community, the heart of which today lies in Plaza Nueva,

« Playa de las Ventanitas
‹ Mojácar. Panoramic View

with its magnificent vantage point looking out over the valley of the Valle de las Pirámides. Just a stone's throw away, next to the monument to the women of Mojácar, is the fortress-like Church of Santa María, which was built in 1560 by Sebastián Segura. Another iconic place is the City Gate, a vast arch dating from 1574 that led into the walled enclosure, and the Casa del Torreón, where tolls to enter the town were once collected. An excellent way to conclude a visit to Mojácar is to climb up to its highest point, where the ruins of a 13th-century castle have been transformed into a vantage point with panoramic views out to sea.

Along its 17 kilometres of shore, Mojácar not only has two ancient coastal watchtowers—the Torre del Peñón (16th century) and the Torre de Macenas (18th century)—on its beach, but lots of places where you can enjoy the sea in total communion with nature, from the long beaches on the Paseo Mediterráneo promenade to the secluded Bordenares and El Sombrerico beaches.

◄ *The Fuente Mora fountain*
Monument to the Women ►
of Mojácar

▴ *Arch in Plaza Nueva*

Vantage point in Plaza Nueva ▸

◄ Southern slope of Mojácar

‹ *Gate to the city*

▴ *Torre de Macenas*

Playa del Sombrerico ›

▲ *Playa del Sombrerico*

Torre del Peñón ▸

Playa del Sombrerico ▸

TURRE AND SIERRA CABRERA

Just a few kilometres from Mojácar, near the Aguas River, is Turre, a town whose houses spread out across a hillock, at the top of which is the Shrine of St. Francis of Assisi. From this highpoint, there are magnificent views out over the rooftops of the town, notable among them the mass of the Parish Church of La Purísima Concepción, built in the late 19th century. Turre makes the ideal starting point for a foray into the Sierra Cabrera, which rises to 900 metres at its highest point and has woodland made up of pines and holm oak. The hills are home to two housing developments: El Cortijo Grande, designed with golf in mind, and Cabrera, a very peaceful place with a markedly Eastern air.

‹ Church of La Purísima Concepción

▾ Public fountain

▴ Calle Nueva

Sierra Cabrera ▸

‹ *Residential development at Cabrera*
‹ *Shrine at La Carrasca*

▴ *La Carrasca,*
a small hamlet in
Sierra Cabrera

GARRUCHA

After Almería, Garrucha is the second most important fishing port in the province. It is famous for its red prawns, which must be sampled in one of the restaurants on the Paseo Marítimo promenade, which has an impressive 1.5-kilometre-long handrail made of Macael marble. The town had a prosperous industrial past and hence has commercial docks that were once kept busy by the numerous mining operations on the Almerian Levante but which are now reduced to shipping out gypsum from Sorbas. Ever since that glorious period, when wealthy families from inland areas would come here for their summer holidays, tourism has been and remains one of the fundamental pillars of the local economy.

▾ *Jesús Nazareno Battery*

Fishing port ▸

⌃ *Preparing fish bait*

Fisherman repairing his nets ›

Promenade with Macael marble handrail

VERA

The city that once stood here was reduced to rubble by a terrible earthquake on 9 November 1518 and so had to be rebuilt in its entirety. As a result, the Vera we see today dates from the 16th century. The Town Hall, which houses the Museum of Ethnography and Archaeology, stands on Plaza Mayor next to the Church of Nuestra Señora de la Encarnación, which was built in 1520 and designed in the manner of a fortress, with bastions at each of the corners of its rectangular floor plan. On the road out of the town heading towards Garrucha stands the prettiest bullring in the entire province, built in 1879. The Vera coast, which includes the Puerto Rey, Las Marinas and El Playazo beaches, has been famous for some years as a naturist area.

- *Residencial Las Marinas*

El Playazo ›
Bullring ›

CUEVAS DE ALMANZORA

This town takes its name from the fact that it stands on the banks of the Almanzora River and from the large number of troglodyte dwellings excavated during the Middle Ages. In addition to its town centre, which is home to the finest castle in El Levante and the important church, the true attraction of the municipality of Cuevas de Almanzora is its stretch of coastline, which is scattered with remains from the old mining operations and splendid spots for communing with the sea, such as the coves of Cala del Peñón Cortado, Cala Invencible and Calón. The town also has a small marina in Villaricos, a notable feature of which is the defensive tower dating from the 18th century.

▾ *Castle of the Marquises of Los Vélez*

◂ *Cave dwellings in El Calguerín*

Cuevas de Almanzora ▸

▲ *Torre de Villaricos*

‹ *Church of Nuestra Señora de la Encarnación*
‹ *Street market*

Remains of the mines at »
El Puntazo de los Ratones and
the marina at Villaricos
Playa Dolores »

Cala del Peñón Cortado ‣

SAN JUAN DE LOS TERREROS

This town in the municipality of Pulpí is the first population centre that a traveller from the coast of Murcia will come to. A tourist town has grown up around a series of cave dwellings once lived in by fishermen. The most prized feature of the town is its castle built during the 18th century on a large hill. From its artillery platform there is a sweeping 180° panoramic view of the coast, from the Carboneras lighthouse of the Cabo Cope in Murcia. Out to sea beyond the peaceful beaches of San Juan de Terreros, notable among them the Playa de Cocedores , are the two islands of Terreros and Negra, which have been declared Natural Sites due to their ecological importance.

‹ Playa de la Rabiosa

‣ Castle of San Juan de los Terreros

▲ *Playa de los Cocedores*

Playa de la Rabiosa ▸

SORBAS

This town renowned for its pottery perches on the edge of a meseta with a tremendous drop, its houses seemingly hanging out over the void, making an impressive sight. The urban layout is, of course, Arab and the town features a number of seigniorial mansions from the 18th and 19th centuries, such as the residences of the Duke de Alba and the Marquis del Carpio next to the Church of Santa Maria, which ingeniously combines the Baroque with Mudéjar and Neoclassical architecture. Sorbas is famous for its Gypsum Karst Natural Beauty Spot, one of the largest karst formations in the world, where it is possible to admire numerous formations of stalactites and stalagmites, some of which have joined to form columns, curtains and walls with extraordinary forms.

▾ *Source of the Aguas River*

Houses in El Tajo ▸

*▴ Tumulus, a karst formation caused
by the washing away of the layer
of gypsum closest to the surface*

*Entrance to a cave of karst origin ▸
Cave in the gypsum karst ▸▸
Juan Simón in his workshop with some ▸▸▸
of the pieces he makes*

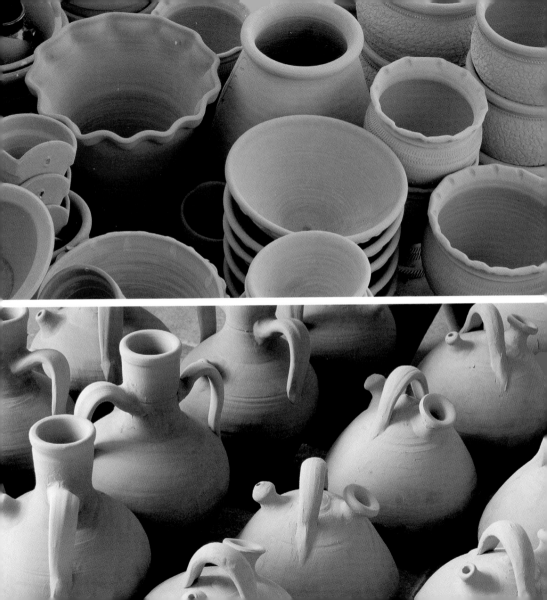

CABO DE GATA-NÍJAR NATURAL PARK

Capricious nature, helped a little by the hand of man, has slowly moulded the arid Cabo de Gata, gradually giving the cape its present-day beauty and biodiversity. To walk these ochre lands is to explore a small universe of volcanic origin with highly singular flora and fauna, sheer cliffs, vantage points with dramatic panoramic views, beaches with unprecedented forms, fortresses from the 18th century, lonely landscapes in which to wander, a hospitable people and a brilliant vernacular architecture.

Protected as a natural park by the Government of Andalusia in 1987 and declared a biosphere reserve ten years later by UNESCO, this paradise stretches across 38,000 hectares of land and 12,000 hectares of sea in which harmony and silence reign. The harsh bioclimatic conditions and the lack of good transport communications have hampered its development, keeping its population low and its beaches virtually unspoiled. In recent years, paradoxically, just when it has achieved its maximum official protection, the park's small towns have experienced unprecedented growth: nothing has escaped the fever to lay bricks, a scourge affecting more and more of the Almerian coast.

The fascinating orography of Cabo de Gata is due to a huge volcanic process in the Tertiary Period, the evidence of which was gently moulded by the sedimentary beds subsequently laid down by the sea as it advanced and receded, giving rise to a relief of sinuous forms in which the occasional volcanic cone can be easily identified, and to a steep coast with cliffs, coves and beaches where spectacular lava formations reveal themselves. The hard subdesert climate and certain economic activities, such as salt extraction, are the main factors that have turned the Cabo de Gata-Níjar into a biogeographical redoubt of tremendous importance. The flora listed here includes more than a thousand species, some of them indigenous such as the Cape Snapdragon (*Antirrhinum charidemi*) and the Cape Carnation (*Dianthus charidemi*). The park also contains a wealth of marine and land fauna, in particular the more than 800 species of birds that can be seen in the park throughout the year, with the pink flamingo (*Phoenicopterus ruber roseus* and the Common Shag (*Phalacrocorax aristotelis*) among the most eye-catching.

◀ *Field of agaves in Las Amoladeras*

Arrecife del Dedo reef in Cala Raja ▶

NÍJAR

Even though the town itself lies outside the protected area, the municipal boundaries encompass almost the entire natural park. This municipality covers 600 square kilometres, making it the third largest in Spain. Famous for the quality of its pottery and its rugs, Níjar's most important monument is the Church of Santa María de la Encarnación. The essence of its past is to be found in the neighbourhood of La Atalaya, made up of a series of steep streets crowned by a lookout tower of Arab origin that offers sweeping views out over the Campos de Níjar and the coast, where the eye is ineluctably drawn to the vast plastic mass of the numerous greenhouses there. A visit to Huebro, a charming country house on the outskirts in the Sierra Alhamilla is not to be missed.

▾ *La Atalaya watchtower*

155

‹ ▲ *Greenhouses in Campos de Níjar*

▴ *Displaying a rug*

⌃ *Loli and her granddaughter painting pottery*

▲ *Picking tomatoes in Campos de Níjar*

▴ Gathering olives near Huebro

▴ *Terraces on Rambla de Huebro*

◂ *Huebro*

A shepherd and his
grandson in Huebro

SAN MIGUEL DE CABO DE GATA

Before heading into the park, it is worth visiting the Las Amoladeras Nature Interpretation Centre to find out about the heritage you are about to discover. The centre stands in an extensive agave plantation next to Playa de Torre García, a beach noted for the 18th-century watchtower from which it takes its name, a shrine of Eastern aspect and the remains of premises where salted foods were produced during Roman times. The charms of San Miguel de Cabo de Gata, a small fishing village attached to the city of Almería, lie in its surroundings, which include the longest beach in the park, and the Salinas, a vast wetland where salt is extracted and a popular spot for lovers of ornithology, who will be able to spot more than 80 species of birds here over the course of the year. Continue southwards and you come to the Cabo de Gata lighthouse after La Almadraba de Monteleva, where the entrance to the saltworks is located, watched over by the pointed bell tower of the mysterious church of the saltworks premises. From its belevedere, there is a breathtaking view of the Arrecife de las Sirenas, which owes its origins to a volcanic chimney. and its name to an old legend. Up until 1974, the reef was occupied by a colony of monk seals, whose calls made sailors uneasy as they were unaware of the existence of the animal and so associated the cries with the songs of sirens. Not far off is another attractive reef, known as El Dedo, on which the Torre de la Vela Blanca stands. This watchtower was built in the 18th century and looks out over La Media Luna, Mónsul and Los Genoveses beaches, which can only be reached on foot.

The church of La Almadraba ▸ de Monteleva

*Saltworks at La Almadraba ▸
de Monteleva*

Playa de San Miguel ▸
on Cabo de Gata

‹ *Old salt-loading machinery in La Almadraba de Monteleva*

La Almadraba de Monteleva ›
Torre García ›

⌐ *The saltworks at La Almadraba de Monteleva*

▲ Flamingos at the saltworks at La Almadraba de Monteleva

*The saltworks at ›
La Almadraba de
Monteleva*

▲ *Lighthouse on Cabo de Gata*

▲ *De las Sirenas reef*

SAN JOSÉ

To reach San José, you first have to cross Pozo de los Frailes, a shantytown with an old noria water wheel that used to supply water to the area. San José, which lies between the hills of En Medio and Cala la Higuera, was once a fishing village but is now the main tourist centre in the park. It makes the best starting point for drives to some of the most extraordinary places on Cabo de Gata such as Campillo de los Genoveses, a vast swathe of open land watched over by an old windmill, and the inlet of the same name; the Playa de Mónsul, a beach with impressive forms and a huge dune leading down to it; the welcoming Playa de la Media Luna; and the secluded coves of El Barronal and Carbón.

‹ Panoramic view

◂ Noria waterwheel at Pozo de los Frailes

▲ *Pozo de los Frailes*

Pozo de los Frailes

▴ *Mill near Pozo de los Frailes*

▲ *Playa de San José*

Playa de Mónsul ‣

▲ *Playa de Mónsul*

Mónsul dune ▸

▲ *Playa de la Media Luna*

◄ *Mónsul dune*

‹ ▲ *Ensenada de los Genoveses*

▴ *Shepherd on Campillo de los Genoveses*
◂ *Cortijo de los Genoveses*

*Windmill on Campillo ▸
de los Genoveses*

ISLETA DEL MORO
AND LOS ESCULLOS

Isleta del Moro, situated on a tiny peninsula next to a small island, is a natural anchorage used for many centuries. Its name apparently comes from a Berber chief who controlled the place. This fishing village might look less charming during the daytime due to the new constructions that never cease to spring up, but it has a highly nostalgic flavour of the sea and two marvellous places for swimming, Playa del Peñón Blanco and Cala de los Toros.

In the environs of the Isleta del Moro, and under the watchful eye of the Cerro del Fraile, is Los Escullos, a small country estate that is home to San Felipe Castle (18th century), which stands on a large fossil dune, and the splendid El Arco and El Esparto beaches.

▾ *Cerro del Fraile viewed from Isleta del Moro*

Isleta del Moro ▸

Isleta del Moro

▲ 22

Los Escullos with Cerro del Fraile and San Felipe Castle in the background

▴ *San Felipe Castle*

▲ *Playa del Arco*

*Panoramic view from ▸
La Amatista vantage
point*

INLAND

The towns and villages along the coast may be experiencing growth due to tourism, but inland there are a number of villages and farms, some outside the protected area of the park, that retain the essence of this land. In these places it is possible to observe the true vernacular architecture of the Cabo de Gata, with its characteristic minimalist forms and highly ingenious design to make the most of the limited water in the area. Los Albaricoques, Fernán Pérez, Las Hortichuelas, La Cortijada de los Martínez, La Cortijada de los Jiménez and the abandoned Cortijo del Fraile, among others, are places that exude a sense of authenticity. To stroll or drive through inland Almería is to travel back to a past that is gradually and silently disappearing.

▾ *House and pond in Los Albaricoques*

Path that crosses ▸
El Hornillo

▲ Los Albaricoques and the remains of an old mill

Cyclists riding past a pond ▸
Traditional houses ▸

‹ *Cortijo del Fraile*

RODALQUILAR

This former settlement built by and for the mining industry turned into a ghost town when the mines closed in the 1960s. Thanks to tourism, however, Rodalquilar has risen from the ashes. Now it is the administrative centre of the park and is home to a botanical garden. The ruins of the old mining village are gradually being done up and the facilities where the material extracted from the mountain was treated to obtain gold are shown with pride. Nearby is the immense El Playazo beach, reached via a broad avenue dotted with palm trees that takes you past the ruins of an ancient Arab fortress. On the beach stands the Castle of San Ramón, which is similar in structure and date to the Castle of Los Escullos.

‣ The church in Rodalquilar

‹ Mines: waste material treated with cyanide piled up into tips

El Playazo with the Castle of San Ramón in the background ▸

Stretch of coast near ▸
El Playazo

Fishermen on El Playazo

LAS NEGRAS

This small village, which owes its name to the impressive hill Cerro Negro, which it lies next to, was once an almost unspoiled paradise but is now a vast tourist development that seems to know no limits. Nevertheless, it retains a special charm in its original houses down by the sea, where the fishermen continue to leave their boats, bringing them up onto the volcanic bombs and dark sands of the beach. To the east of the village behind Cerro Negro is the quiet cove of Cala de San Pedro, an idyllic spot that can only be reached by boat or after a two-hour walk. The cove has a freshwater spring and is watched over by the ruins of the castle from which it takes its name.

▾ *Cove and Castle of San Pedro*

Playa de Las Negras ▸

AGUA AMARGA

This peaceful fishing village nestles in a small cove at the foot of the hill on which stand the ruins of an old loading platform where mineral from the Lucainena and Las Torres mines was transported from. Today it has become an urban nucleus where increasing numbers of second homes are springing up. The surrounding coast has two perfect spots for going for a dip: the Cala de Enmedio, a cove situated in a marvellous spot with crystal-clear water that can only be reached on foot and is flanked by sheer rock faces that give it a somewhat surrealist air (it seems to be the work of Salvador Dalí himself); and the Cala del Plomo, another attractive cove that can be reached by car along a dirt track.

▾ Off to catch squid

Cala del Plomo ▸

Cala de Enmedio ▸

CARBONERAS

Carboneras, which lies on the slopes of the Sierra Cabrera, looking out towards the Isla de San Andrés, is the main port in the north-east of the park. It developed in the 17th century around the Castle of San Andrés, which the Marquis del Carpio had built to defend his land from pirate invasions. Carboneras separated administratively from Sorbas in 1837. Even though it has a small industrial estate, consisting basically of a small cement factory and a thermal power station with a frightful tower, much of this municipality lies within the natural park, where it has some impressive spots, such as the beaches of Los Muertos and El Algarrobico, the Mesa Roldán tower and the Mesa Roldán lighthouse.

‹ Mesa Roldán lighthouse

▾ Cruz de las Misiones

▴ *Playa del Ancón with Isla de San Andrés in the background*

▴ *Battery at La Mesa Roldán*

Playa de los Muertos ▸